CHAPLAIN
Reflective Spaces

A journal for writing

Copyright © 2020 by CHAPLAIN SHARON

All rights reserved. No part of this book may be reproduced or used in any manner without written permission of the copyright owner except for the use of quotations
in a book review.

Quotations in this work derive from the thoughts and inspiration of the author and were not directly quoted from any outside sources.

Chaplain Life

www.chaplainlife.org
www.chaplaingear.com

Follow us on Social Media
Twitter/IG/Facebook @chaplaingear
Tag us with #chaplaingear #chaplainlife

Space

There is individuality and autonomy in certain spaces. Space can be freedom, inspiration, vision. May these pages serve as a space of what you desire and need them to be for you.

Peace and Compassion,
Chaplain Sharon

Generosity is a gift that may yield the unseen.

The gift of you is unique enough.

Chaplains operate beyond boxes.

Boxes are often too small anyway.

When days are difficult, may you be reminded of your inspirational source(s).

Sometimes people tell chaplains what they will tell no one else. You are trustworthy indeed.

<u>Replenishing the soul is like a refreshing wind that energizes one to lift the arms, tilt the head back, and bask in its refreshing benefits.</u>

CHAPLAINS DESERVE SELF-CARE.

**Someone loves you.
You're a chaplain!**
♥

One of the most beautiful things to wear can simply be a smile. ☺

Intuition is a powerful tool. Trust it.

Bring to the world, your best and authentic self.

Chaplains often emanate compassion in the most difficult circumstances.

> **Emotions are like keys, unlocking a world of information about ourselves and others. Access them.**

Achieving greater balance is often individual and unique.

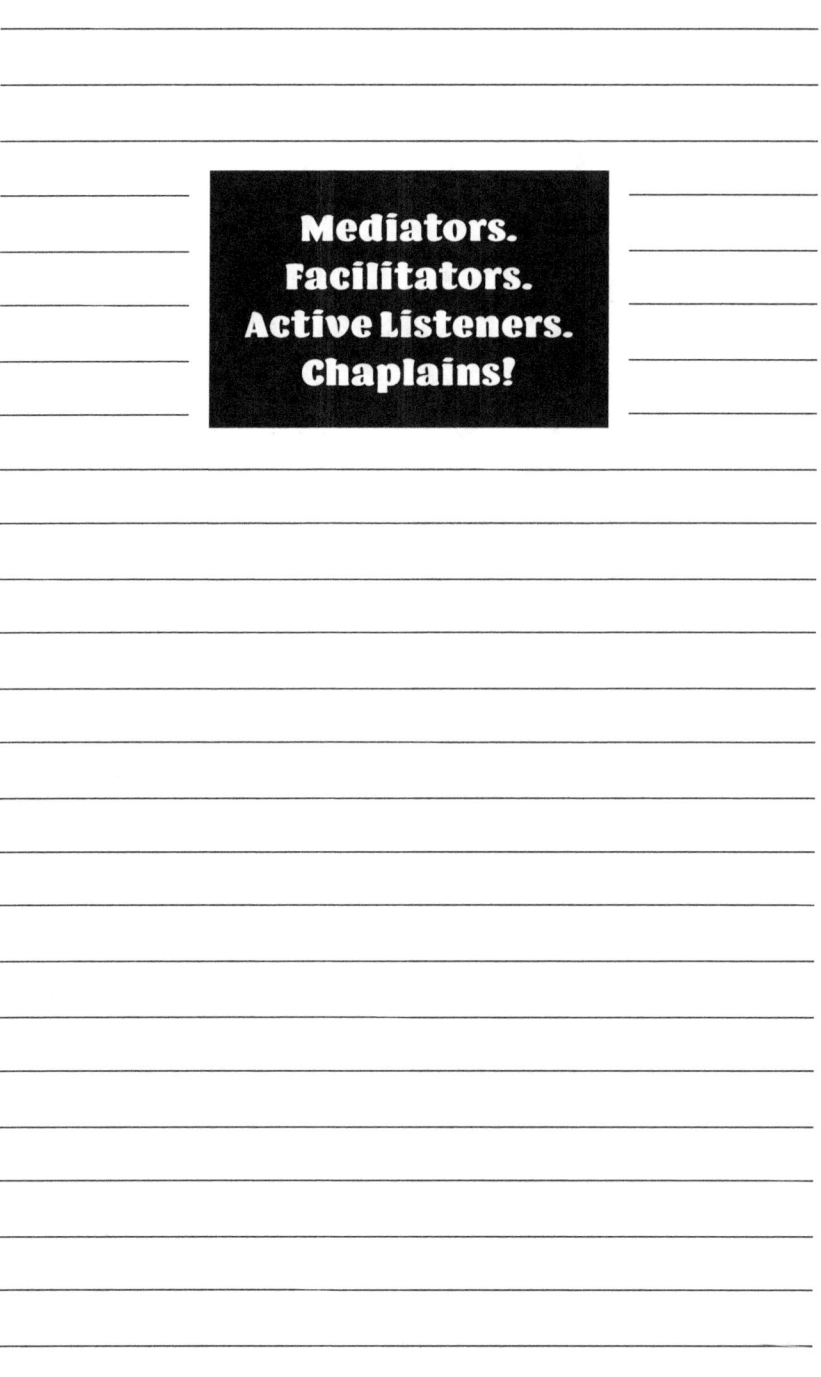

DREAMS AND VISIONS ARE WORTHY OF OUR ATTENTION.

LAUGH.

       SMILE.

              REJOICE.

Thank you for being a Chaplain

www.ingramcontent.com/pod-product-compliance
Lightning Source LLC
Chambersburg PA
CBHW071403080526
44587CB00017B/3171